Rifflets

(and other ekphrases)

bob rj canuel

PRAIRIE SOUL PRESS

PRAIRIE SOUL PRESS

Cover credit: Giancarlo Duarte on Unsplash

ISBN-13: 978-1-7779474-0-8

To all
the artists
in this world
of every sort,
in every when
and every where,
a tip of the hat
from scribes and players
you ignite

Contents

Definitions

riff·let

| rif·lət |

noun from the root '**riff**' [1930s, perhaps an abbreviation of *refrain*]

1. a short poem inspired by music or a lyric and often consisting of sixty words or less in two 8-line stanzas with limited punctuation

ek·phra·sis

| ek·phra·sis | \ ˈek-frə-səs |

noun [variants, or less commonly, *ecphrasis*]

plural ekphrases al-so ecphrases\ ˈek- frə- ˌsēz]

1. a literary description of, or commentary on, a visual work of art
2. a poem of any length, in any style, inspired by a work of art such as, but not limited to, a line or lines from written works of prose or poetry, a song, a lyric, a photo, a sculpture or a painting

Rifflets

Inspired by Joanna Newsom's
Divers, *2015*

BEAR YOUR BROKEN SOLDIER

he's weary
to the bone
and hope
lies
wounded,
bleeding
and burned
with hot lead

fired
by broken politics
and boy-men
caught
in the maw
of war
and profit
unbound

BRAVE MEN AND WOMEN, SO DEAR TO GOD

isn't it
the Way
of the Word
that we're all
so dear to Him
that death
and forever
are ours

if only
surrender
could explain
divinity
and help us
understand
His eagerness
to punish

SOMEBODY BURNS

in merry lays
of war
and celebration,
their songs
of home
and hearth
were sad
while fragile

hearts with eyes
begged
far horizons
for the safe
return
of their men
from red,
red fields

AND THE WAR HAD BEGUN

without trying,
we'd fallen
into trenches
and dismemberment
and prayed
to the gods
of war
we might survive

the bullets
and bombs
specially prepared
to separate
limb from limb
and dull
the eyes
of lambs

WITH THE ICE IN YOUR LUNGS

with the ice
in your lungs
and hearts
banging
to stay
alive
at night,
alone

and wordless
in a dream,
you wander
all about
and scamper
from one
interment
to another

BLEEDING OUT YOUR DAYS

on a chair
in the green garden,
an ancient
father
of two
wiles away
the morning
as old blood

courses
through his veins
and tries to ease
the passing
of life
bleeding
from one day
to a last

Inspired by Van Morrison's
"Moondance," 1970

AND MAYHEM THEIR GOD

"we were born before the wind,"
spry and wise
beyond the years
of long and slow
and songs
of hurt and hollow
that plied the stations
all around us

as we rocked and we rolled
among the old and the bold
in the court of souls
where we swore the children
made murder
their watchword
and mayhem
their god

Inspired by The Tragically Hip's
"Fully Completely," 1992

FORGOTTEN

maybe changing
the world
was a fool's errand
and we should have
let the bigots
rule
from stone temples
and sit-rooms

but we apprehended
the weight
of history
and what was seen
and heard
and felt
we simply could not
disregard

Inspired by Emily Barker & the Red Clay Halo's
"Despite the Snow," 2008

OF ANY OTHER ANSWER

a grey street,
dim lit and wet,
where I dragged
myself,
head held
low,
through the grime
of winter

and asked
of no one in particular,
"Who and where am I?"
if not me
and here,
afeared
of any other
answer

OF DIRE DAYS AND DUTY

a curse
spans
generations,
from father
to son,
and hangs
heavy
as a millstone

about the neck
of the well-meant
and forlorn
gone awry
in the blind
and bustle
of dire days
and duty

*Inspired by Jefferson Airplane's
"Surrealistic Pillow," 1967*

NOW LOCKED AND LOADED

a wretched
emptiness
filled
with voices
of polity
and fear
hides clerics
and captains

who strain
to blame
any other
in the land
of pride
and armed
believers,
each locked and loaded

*Inspired by Jim Jackson's
"Flypaper Motel," 2018*

DAYS OF DAMNED AND DIMMING LIGHT

a ragged harp
rips morning
out of shadow
and draws
you into places
where stories
gather,
stories of sinners,

saints
and preacher men
dressed
in black
and conceit,
who protest
the dimming
of the light

I'LL BE LOVING YOU

weeks
and wayward
hearts
still yearn
to love
and learn
the beat
among chords

hard
to name,
let alone
to finger,
as the song
ascends
to loving
you

I'LL SING A SONG FOR SARAH

the girl
sits alone
watches
the band
with a gleam
in her eye
and jiggers
of Cuervo

on the table
with shakers
of salt,
wedges of lime
and blues
anticipating
songs
for Sarah

AND NAMES RETREATED BACK TO SAND

they were days
of deserts
and heat
and spring
floods
that made
gods
and Pharaohs

retreat
to sand
and afterlives
in boats
of papyrus
ladened with food
and wine to ease
their journey

AND THE HEAVY RAIN DEVOURS

while W overflew,
praised Brownie
for FEMA
and Cheney
looked a little
awkward after
being told
to go fuck himself,

Katrina devoured
New Orleans,
levies broke
and flowers
died
in the freshets
that heavy, heavy rain
engenders

WHERE LONESOME HIGHWAYS END

blacktop
and broken lines
across the prairie
seem forever
when you're
alone
behind the wheel
and dead-air-radio

morphs
into preaching
about Jesus
and the cross
while day
descends to night
before your heavy
eyes

AND SHATTERING THE SUN

children
at the cold,
cold lake,
frolic
in the sun
and laugh
at bird games
of high-fun,

fish and feathers
that hang
in the wind
before darting
down to break
the calm
of a millpond-sea
and shattering the sun

Inspired by Sigur Rós's
Valtari, 2012

NEW SHORES

the day
began
as usual
when the earth
melted
before their eyes
and burned
to ash

any little
homes
that blocked
the path
to a steaming
northern sea
where new land
cooled

AND TITILLATE

it was crowded
at the inn
when the unmoored
and weary
clambered
from the sea
to glory
and wealth

in search
of bed
and drink
in the arms
of servers
dressed
to distract
and titillate

Inspired by Crosby, Stills & Nash's
Crosby Stills & Nash, 1969

OF HISTORY

brown faces
gazed out
with eyes,
so wide
and dark
they held back
time
and asked

in a new language,
"Who are you?"
that I could not
look away or speak
and only pointed
to my ship
at the edge
of history

Inspired by The Doors'
The Doors, 1967

FOR THE NEARLY DEAD

souls rage
behind the wheel,
between night
and day,
heavy
with acceleration
and ready
with tires, glass and steel

for the grim task
set before them
by white line
fevers
and asphalt
that define
a course
for the nearly dead

*Inspired by Ima Robot's
Another Man's Treasure, 2015*

AND ALWAYS RIGHT

custom-shirted
nobility,
in three-piece
suits,
oversold
straw-dogs
and glory-stories
to the hopeful

who blamed
themselves
for the sins
of markets
they believed
were self-correcting,
white
and always right

Inspired by Supertramp's
Crime of the Century, *1974*

MEAN TO STAY AMONG US

watch them
perform
on stages,
left
to right,
and deliver
dialogue
to an audience

that ought
to wonder
what they really
mean to say
and if they
truly
mean to stay
among us

Inspired by Patti Smith's
Horses, 2013

OF OLD BONEYARDS

sun-dry and hot
in a summer's noon,
the smell
of dead cream
stains the breeze
while you search
fields of view
at the edge

of heavy blue
and steel strings
bend,
from high
to low,
with memory stones
and the call
of old boneyards

TO THERE AND EVERYWHERE

air shimmers
from the heat
as your body sways
like an aurora
to a song you can see,
a 21st music
of the spheres,
in space and time

that gathers voices
who yield with a lilt
in their laugh
you can hear
above the sound
of sand in runnels
on their way to there
and everywhere

ALL THE FIRES FROZEN

wounds gather
by the door
and memories burn
in evening's cold
while hearts
in a yellow glow
dream of
far, far down below

where melted rock
presses up
and we finally grasp
how bodies
can remember
when we believe
all the fires
frozen

Poetry

Inspired by Laurie Anne Fuhr

THE LIMBS OF SEEDLING POEMS

"in her West eye,"
mountains rise
from crashing
crustal plates
while their slopes gleam
in new morning suns
beneath forever-blue
skies.

in her East eye,
the plains
spread out
beneath her feet
in tribute
to the sea bottom
that formed there
in eons past.

in her North eye,
the trees grow thin
and tundra
moves across horizons
with the sound
of caribou
in their march

of seasons.

while in her South eye,
the green
grows thick
and heavy
like leaf duvets
to warm
the limbs
of seedling poems.

Inspired by Weyman Chan

FOR BETTER OUTCOMES

*"and the new day is
only one more bomb away"*
where America
can fear again
because they know
patriots
within their borders
cut out
the eyes
and ears
of any threat
they find
while machines
and kerosene
deliver
fabled munitions
to a world
twisted
with exception
and the shock
of collaterals
who watch
this folly
become new religion

and hymns
become burnt offerings
to gods
of disorder
where fools
take up arms
for grey men
in portraits
mounted
on the walls
of holy halls
and black robes
deliberate,
in quiet,
while the sad,
the lonely
and the woebegone
wait
in vain
for better outcomes.

Inspired by Richard Oslerr

TO FELL

"so many ways,
at night,
to drown."

so many brows,
by might,
to crown.

so many hours,
each day,
to spend.

so many smiles,
and ways,
to mend.

so many songs,
of youth,
to sing.

so many bells,
in truth,
to ring.

so many states,
of fear,
to heal.

so many fates,
my dear,
to seal.

so many tales,
of woes,
to tell.

so many schemes,
of foes,
to fell.

Inspired by Vivian Hansen

PROUD AND MIGHTY KINGS

*"Pain
begins in these fields"*

of red, black-centred poppy
that hears voices whisper
of the lost.

And though every generation since
attests the wounds of folly
never healed,

the haze of history,
chiseled into stones of grief,
sells men and women short

who commanded by the crown
now remember limbs and bodies
offered to their greater god.

So pray again,
my ardent friends,
that any sacrifice to come

can satisfy
the hungry hopes
of cenotaphs-to-be

and fill the maw,
of light made into night,
with fated choices,

bleak and blue,
of fealty to
proud and mighty kings.

Inspired by Clara A.B. Joseph

BEYOND PRIZE

What is the weight,
"the worth of a word."
in a deluge
of words?

You might as well ask
if a tsunami
cares what it engulfs.

But a single word,
a chosen word,
strained
with care
from the master book,
selected
by a third ear
or a third eye,
a perfect word,
resonant,
that captures
the soft murmur
of the muse
and your surrender,
discernible

in the clamour
of a million voices,

is beyond prize
and ever rare
for poets
in their lairs
or market squares.

OF SOULS ALONE LIKE ME

*"Once upon a midnight dreary, while I pondered,
weak and weary"*
On phantoms, ghosts and varied wraiths of good and
ill,
A lady fair reminded me, I did foreswear
The easy lure of drink that months and years fade,
And the mindless wishes of early evening shade
When blinds are tightly drawn.

The inebriated staggered, like a wealthy, drunken
laggard,
Across the covered stoops to heat and hearth inside
Where coat and scarf forgot what cold and night had
wrought,
How spectral hours waited for baited breath to ease,
And midnight's little light had shed its breath, to please
The dream before it died.

And when comfort sat astride the chair, in that dark
and thirsty lair,
I burned my offerings to daemons of the night,
And glass held high, accompanied by slurred good-
byes,
I caught the candle's gleam and the ears of witches,

Like sordid songs overheard in times of bitches,
How sense escaped my gaol.

Then with the dawn of yellow day, dull headed,
bleary-eyed and fey,
I wondered what had filled the mem'ry holes just
made
That out of bliss, I knew that something was amiss;
A stuporous me had kneeled in hazy masses,
Far from afterworlds in alcoholic classes,
Where wights preyed upon me

And satisfied their hunger raw with raven's beak and
reddened claw
In a fetid feast of mortal flesh afflicted,
I walked out to the street, on barely able feet,
And saw the working boys and painted, high-heeled
toys
Lean up against the walls amidst the low-browed noise
Of souls alone like me.

Photos

Inspired by A Stump, Ontario, 2015

OF LIFE

It's a tall stump,
now grey
and clear
eyed,

watchful of
chicory blue
roadsides
and canola-yellow

fields
tended each summer
by families
with old names,

familiar
to local
graveyards,
whose generations

revered
the seasons,
the value
of land,

hard work
and the rise
and fall
of life.

Inspired by A Doll's Head at the Titanic Wreck

OF OUR 20TH

it's a moment
of pause
for breath

unheeded
by the empty
eyes

in the face
of a porcelain
doll's head

at the bottom
of the North
Atlantic,

a relic
of steam
and revolution

in the late 19th
and the start
of the 20th

Inspired by Katie Green and daniel j. kirk's
The Imaginarium

FOR AGES STILL TO COME

The wall
has visions
and hands
and life aplenty,
where artists
indulged
a fondness
for birds
cupped
in hands
or astride
the face
of an eye
or a deer,
while in the heart
of that mural,
a beating
for the ages
that almost moves
with a warm
and sexual
assembly
of skin

and legs
in a beautiful
joining
for ages
still to come

Inspired by Carmina Trsic's
An Untitled Ink Drawing

IN THE READING

Her voice spills
lines
about her legs
that cling there,
like dampness
does to skin,
with inks
that blend
one
to the other.

Her face,
in profile,
she gazes
at the poem
in her hand,
like a sceptre,
as she reads
to sovereign muses
hovering about her
on the air.

Other Music

Inspired by Toundra's
IV, 2015

TO RIGHT AND LEFT

A band
of young men,
          Spanish men,
whose music
holds me
in thrall again,
          spawns another verse
          from Sunday,
with jagged chords,
          like broken glass,
that ply the air
of a digital world
with sounds
and rhythms
that capture
the ears
and eyes
of a scribe
entranced
by lines
that splay
and splutter
from his fingers

to a page
bereft
until it's filled
with reflections,
      on guitar
      or drums
      or brass,
that can make
even old shoes smile
in decades
clambering
up the walk
of closing time
where pillars
of salt
appear
to right
and left.

Inspired by John Martyn's
Excuse Me, Mister, *1998*

FOUR YEARS GONE AND MISSED

It's morning
and I'm tethered
to a song
again.

There's wonderful guitar
in there
with heavy hooks
but it's his voice
that holds me fast
within its grasp.

It pleads
and rolls
like gravel
on glass
through verse
after verse
with a measured phrasing
by a practiced
and careful poet
of song

now more than four years gone
and missed.

Inspired by Donovan's
A Gift from a Flower to a Garden, *1967*

WEAR YOUR LOVE LIKE HEAVEN

"wear your love like heaven"
and kiss me,
touch me
in the flutter
of a ragged flag
and lose me to a song.

let me rest
in your arms,
forget
the hues
of Prussian blue
in night and fog.

let me linger
in the dream
and taste the wines
and wherefores
of loss or leader
before the stores are closed.

and be as quick to laugh as frown,
at faces all around,

and cheer the songs and singers
who demand your guards are down
when you're asked to sing along
as if no one else was listening.

THE DANGLING CONVERSATION

Words hang
in the dry air
between lovers
set adrift
on dust
colliding
with sunlight
passing through
a dirty summer
window.

They dance
and dangle
in the sun
before merging
into night
and memory
where they loop
in effortless
review
till dawn.

The exchange
seems almost done,
before begun,
as minutes
pass unseen
through hope
to the dusk
of western smokes
and red-sun mornings
above Calgary.

So keep to the path,
lover friends,
and pray the gods
are inattentive
when the door closes
on her heart
and screen doors
keep hungry summer's
flies
at bay.

Inspired by Glenn Gould's
Bach: the Goldberg Variations, *1955*

WITHOUT THE NEED OF WORDS

I'm listening
to Glenn, again,
and swaying

as if a wind
blew
through the room.

Music can do that to me;
      it's the closest
      I've ever come

      to poetry
      without the need
      of words.

LIGHTNING CRASHES

"forces pullin'
from the centre of the earth
again"

like magma
though rocky crust
where hoary words

rise up and grab
my dreams
like gravity

and never ever
let me
alone

with silver ice
or baby's breath
that might deflect

the morbid
attentions

of the glib

and garish
who parade
themselves

as symbols
of desire
and objects

of envy
by souls, like mine,
who only shrug.

Acknowledgements

Setting aside the obvious thanks to all the musicians, composers, artists, photographers and poets credited in this volume, some further acknowledgments are still needed.

"And Mayhem Their God" was published online by the Alexandra Writers' Centre Society in 2018. "Proud and Mighty Kings" was included in *The War Memory Project* from the Alexandra Writers' Centre Society scheduled for 2019. My thanks to AWCS for their continuing support.

Thanks, and the deepest appreciation, are also extended to fellow poets, prosers and artists including Jim Jackson, of course, Laurie Ann Fuhr, Chris Evans, Adrienne Adams, Vivian Hansen, Kirk Miles, Wakefield Brewster, Miranda Krogstad, Richard Harris, Igpy Kin, Weyman Chan, Josephine LoRe, Pam Medland, Paul Swift, Micheline Maylor, Josh Forbes, Nina Alvarez, Kirk Miles, Wendy Miles and so many, many others who have provided encouragement and advice, whether they were aware of it or not.

And finally, my deepest appreciation to Bev, my wife, for years of love and support of my poetry. And a special thanks to my daughter, Robin, and her husband, Tim, for their continuing help and support.

Manufactured by Amazon.ca
Bolton, ON

27376241R00044